Space

Written by Sarah Powell
Designed by Nicola Friggens
and Katherine Radcliffe

priddy books
big ideas for little people

The Universe is mind-bogglingly big. It is everything that exists — every speck of dust, rock, planet, solar system, and galaxy. It is difficult to imagine just how big the Universe is, that's because we think it's infinite or never-ending, containing an unimaginable number of stars!

This is a nebula, where new stars and galaxies are made

This huge cosmic pillar is made of hydrogen and dust

The Universe

The Milky Way

A black hole is thought to exist in the middle

Galaxies come in all different shapes. This one is a spiral

We are somewhere here!

The Milky Way is just one of the **billions** of galaxies that exist in the known **Universe,** and it is also home to our Solar System. It is called a **spiral** galaxy, due to its shape, and contains between 200-400 billion stars (like the Sun), and some 50 billion planets!

The asteroid belt
is between Mars
and Jupiter

The closest
to the Sun

The Sun

Mercury

The perfect
conditions
for life

Earth

Venus

It's the
hottest planet

Mars

The Solar System is where
we call home. The Sun is
in the middle of the Solar System,
and everything else orbits around it.
There are a total of eight planets, some with
their own moons, as well as five dwarf planets,
including Pluto. The Earth is the third planet
closest to the Sun, with Neptune being the furthest.

Has a
volcano
bigger than
Mt. Everest

The Solar System

Jupiter

The biggest planet

Saturn

Rings of ice and dust

uranus

Has 27 moons

Winds blow at 1,200 mph (1,930 km/h)

Neptune

Until very recently there were nine planets in our Solar System. But in 2006 scientists took away Pluto's planet status. It is now a minor planet, or dwarf planet. Poor Pluto!

Smaller than some moons in the Solar System, Mercury is the planet **closest** to the Sun. It looks very similar to the surface of our moon, and is covered in **craters** made when huge **asteroids** crashed into its surface. Mercury is so dense, it has a large core made of pure **molten** iron!

The side of Mercury which faces the Sun is up to 10 times hotter than Earth

Heat from the Sun

Mercury has one of the largest impact craters in the Solar System

Mercury

Venus

It was once thought that Venus was similar to Earth, and that **life** might even exist there, but we were very wrong. In fact it is the most **unfriendly** planet in the Solar System! Its surface **temperature** is so hot it could melt lead, its air is mainly composed of **carbon dioxide**, and there are layers of poisonous sulphuric **acid** clouds in its atmosphere.

Venus is the brightest planet in our skies

It is sometimes called Earth's "sister planet"

Its diameter is only 400 miles (644 km) less than that of Earth's

Key facts:
Order from the Sun: 2nd
Size: Nearly the same size as Earth
Number of moons: 0
Type: Terrestrial planet

Earth

Earth is the only known planet in our Solar System with life. We call Earth the Blue Planet because of the oceans that cover most of the surface. The Earth takes 24 hours to rotate on its axis, giving us day and night, and 365 days to orbit the Sun, giving us changes in seasons.

The ozone layer protects us from the Sun's harmful rays

The Moon orbits the Earth

Oceans cover 70% of the Earth's surface

Key facts:
Order from the Sun: 3rd
Size: 5th largest
Number of moons: 1
Type: Terrestrial planet

Mars

Mars is known as the **Red Planet.** It is the planet that is most like Earth, although as it is further from the Sun it is very **cold.** Scientists have discovered **ice** beneath its surface. This may mean that **life** once existed there! One day we hope humans will set foot on it!

Mars' red shade is made by iron in the planet's surface

Huge craters, valleys, and mountains cover the surface

Across the middle is the 1,864 mile (3,000 km) long canyon called Valles Marineris

Key facts:
Order from the Sun: 4th
Size: Half Earth's size
Number of moons: 2
Type: Terrestrial planet

On November 13, 1971, Mariner 9 became the first space probe to maintain orbit around another planet, and this was Mars! Exciting pictures and data were beamed back down to Earth.

Jupiter

Jupiter is a very stormy planet with winds of more than 400 mph (644 km/h)

The planet is covered in thick red, brown, yellow, and white clouds

The Great Red Spot is a huge storm three times the size of Earth

Jupiter is the biggest planet in our Solar System. It is so big that it is 2.5 times the size of all the other planets combined! It is made mainly from gas and is known as one of the four gas giants along with Saturn, Uranus, and Neptune.

Key facts:
Order from the Sun: 5th
Size: 1,300 Earths
Number of moons: 64
Type: Gas giant

Jupiter's four largest moons

Io   Europa   Ganymede   Callisto

Saturn is the **second** largest planet in the Solar System. It has nine beautiful rings that can be seen with a telescope. Its **rings** are made up of **ice, rock, and dust.** Saturn spins very fast on its axis — a day on Saturn lasts only **10 hours.**

Saturn

Key facts:

Order from the Sun: 6th

Size: 764 Earths

Number of moons: 62

Type: Gas giant

Some ring particles are dust-sized, while some are as big as mountains. They are made from comets, asteroids or shattered moons

ROTATION DIRECTION

Uranus is the only planet that rotates on its side

The bright blue color comes from methane gas

Uranus is so far away, that if you were **traveling** there from the Sun, and you made it to Saturn you'd only be half way there! It is a very **cold** place with temperatures reaching as low as -371°F (-224°C) above its **cloud** layer. Little is known about this **distant,** blue planet and what lies beneath its clouds remains a **mystery.**

Uranus

Key facts:
Order from the Sun: 7th
Size: 60 Earths
Number of moons: 27
Type: Gas giant

This is Titania, its biggest moon. It is 980 miles (1,577 km) across.

Neptune

Key facts:
Order from the Sun: 8th
Size: 57 Earths
Number of moons: 13
Type: Gas giant

The **furthest** planet out from the Sun, Neptune is a cold **icy** giant. It is a very bright blue, due to **methane** gas, with a water layer that leads down to a **solid core** the size of Earth. It takes **165 years** to orbit the Sun, meaning that its winter lasts for 40 years!

Voyager 2 is the first and only spacecraft to pass this distant planet

The Great Dark Spot is a storm the size of planet Earth

Its orbit of the Sun takes so long that it has only been around the Sun once since its discovery in 1846

People who watch the skies are called **astronomers.** They use telescopes to study the sky and look at planets, **stars,** and **galaxies,** and cosmic events like supernovas. People have been looking at the stars for thousands of years. It is impossible to imagine just how many stars there are in the **Universe.**

This is the Big Dipper constellation

Many important space discoveries have been made by people using telescopes

Stars

The Sun

This haze is called the corona

The energy from the Sun is called the solar wind

Key facts:
Core temperature: Around 75,000 times hotter than an oven!
Size: 1.3 million Earths
Age: 4.5 billion years old
Gravity: 28 times that of Earth's

The Sun is the star at the middle of our Solar System, that gives us heat, and light for life on Earth. It is a giant burning ball of hydrogen and helium gas, with a surface temperature of 9,932°F (5,500°C). That's **HOT!** The Sun is so big its diameter is 109 times that of Earth's!

Red areas of the Sun are the coolest

Sudden huge explosions of energy are called solar flares

Space Rocks

The crater is 558 ft (170 m) deep

The meteorite crashed on Earth 50,000 years ago

The meteorite that made this crater broke off from a huge asteroid in space

This is the Meteor Crater in Arizona, USA

Famous space rocks

Asteroid Ida is one of the biggest known asteroids. It is so big it has its own moon!

Halley's Comet appears every 75 years. It's the only comet you're likely to see in your lifetime!

Space is home to rocks of all shapes and sizes. There are icy shimmering comets orbiting the Sun, huge irregularly shaped asteroids the size of planets, and meteors that can enter the Earth's atmosphere as shooting stars.

Satellites

Man-made satellites are really **useful.** We use them to monitor space and our **planet.** Orbiting the Earth, they send data and signals back down to satellite **dishes.** Since the first satellite, Sputnik I, was launched in 1957 by Russia, there are now **thousands** of satellites orbiting the Earth.

Incoming signals are received by the curved dish

This satellite dish is located on Earth and communicates with satellites in space

Satellites are used every day

Satellite TV

Mobile devices

Weather reports

Navigation

The Moon

The Moon is a dry, dusty place with no air. It is covered in hollows, called craters, made by huge meteoroids crashing into its surface, which still happens today! Ocean tides on Earth are caused by the Moon's gravitational force. The Moon is the only place in space where humans have landed.

The Moon takes 27 days, 7 hours, 43 minutes, 11.6 seconds to orbit the Earth

The Moon's surface is covered in impact craters

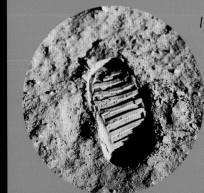

In 1969, Neil Armstrong, an American astronaut, became the first man to walk on the Moon. His footprints from 1969 can still be seen on the Moon's surface today.

Lunar Module carried a crew of two from lunar orbit to the Moon's surface and back

The Moon is an incredible 4.5 billion years old

Space stations are manned satellites that travel in a low orbit of the Earth. They allow astronauts to live and work in space for long periods of time and other spacecraft can dock onto them. The longest serving and biggest space station ever is the International Space Station (ISS).

Solar arrays help power the space station

Launched in 1998

ISS orbits the Earth 16 times a day

The ISS is about the same length as a soccer pitch

On board there is general living space, a gym, and laboratories

Space Station

Exploring Mars

Mars Reconnaissance Orbiter has taken astonishing pictures of its surface

Mars Rovers

In August 2012, the NASA Curiosity Rover became the latest rover to land on Mars. Its mission: to explore the surface, to analyze Martian rocks, and discover if humans can land there one day!

Gullies discovered on the surface of Mars could have been formed by water

In recent years many **rockets** have launched **orbiters**, landers, and rovers into space to study and explore Mars. Four rovers have landed on Mars and **roamed** its surface. They have taken over **300,000** images so far, as well as collected lots of data about Martian rocks.

Rockets

Every space mission begins at mission control, where a team of scientists and engineers prepare to launch a rocket into space. Huge rockets are ignited on a launch pad. The rockets gain enough power to take off, rise up and enter space, climbing over 1,000 ft (300 m) in a few seconds.

This Apollo rocket had a crew of three, seated in the top

Rockets are so powerful they shoot up high into the atmosphere

The biggest rocket ever was Saturn V at over 300 ft (91 m)

Mission Control

Rocket missions are controlled from Earth at mission control. Teams of scientists, engineers, and flight controllers track a rocket's progress from the point of lift off.

Astronauts

Astronauts are **brave** men and women who venture into space. They are sent on special **missions.** Some astronauts have landed on the **Moon,** while others are sent to work on **space stations** orbiting the Earth.

Oxygen supply tank

Protective helmet

This astronaut is out on a space walk

Spacesuit

Key facts:

First in space:
Yuri Gagarin

First on the Moon:
Neil Armstrong

Fastest speed traveled:
Apollo 10 astronauts, 36,440 feet per second (11,107 meters per second)

Most time spent in space:
Gennady Padalka, almost 2.5 years

Longest single stay in space:
Valeri Polyakov, 438 days

The external tank holds fuel for the main engines

Burning fuel creates huge clouds of smoke

The Space Shuttle was the world's first reusable **spacecraft** that carried large satellites to and from orbit around the Earth. It zoomed into space like a **rocket,** sat in Earth's orbit like a spacecraft and then landed back on Earth like an **airplane,** transporting crew and equipment up to space stations such as the **ISS.**

NASA launched its final Space Shuttle in 2011

The Orbiter houses the crew

Space Shuttle

How about a trip into space for your next **vacation?**
It's very possible, with companies like Virgin
Galactic developing new **spacecraft** to do so.
Scientists hope that one day we might
be able to use the same spacecraft to
travel across the world in just **3 hours!**

New Mexico
is home to the
world's first
commercial
spaceport

Passengers will
experience
zero gravity

Space Tourism

Ticket to fly

Tickets for the first
Virgin Galactic flight
are on sale now,
for US $250,000.

Timeline

1608
Hans Lippershey invents the telescope. Galileo later improves this design, and finds proof that the Earth orbits the Sun

1687
Isaac Newton describes his theory of gravity

1846
Neptune is discovered by Johann Galle

1949
Monkeys become the first living mammals to fly into space

1682
Edmond Halley discovers Halley's Comet, which is named after him

1781
William Herschel discovers Uranus

1926
Robert Goddard launches the world's first liquid-fueled rocket

1957
USSR scientists launch the first satellite into space, marking the beginning of the space age

1959
The USSR and America begin a space race to be the first to land on the Moon

1969
American Neil Armstrong is the first man on the Moon followed by Buzz Aldrin

2011
End of Space Shuttle program with final launch of Space Shuttle Atlantis

1990
Hubble Space Telescope launched

1961
USSR astronaut, Yuri Gagarin, becomes the first man in space

1977
Launch of Voyager deep space probes

1998
Construction begins on the International Space Station

And beyond...
How about taking a trip into space on your very own spaceflight?

Glossary

Asteroid A rock, or small Dwarf Planet orbiting the Sun.

Axis An imaginary straight line on which an object rotates.

Black holes A region of space around a very small but extremely massive object, where the gravitational field is so strong that not even light can escape.

Constellation A grouping of stars that have been given names by ancient astronomers because of the way they look.

Dwarf planets Smaller planets that do not meet all the rules to become an official planet.

Gas giants The four big gas planets in our Solar System: Jupiter, Saturn, Uranus, and Neptune.

Moon Something that orbits another object in space, usually a planet.

Nebulae Clouds of gas and dust where new galaxies are made.